GOD, I've Gotta Talk to You... AGAIN!

Prayers FOR children

Prayers for children

Written by Dan Carr and John Paquet
Illustrated by Gordon Willman

ARCH® Books

Copyright © 1985 CONCORDIA PUBLISHING HOUSE

3558 S. Jefferson Avenue, St. Louis, MO 63118-3968

Manufactured in the United States of America

God's Beautiful World

The sky is blue, the grass is green,
    The flowers are in bloom.
The trees reach up into the sky,
    The clouds look like balloons.

I am so happy to be here
    Surrounded by Your love,
For all the things my eyes can see
    Were sent from You above.

I cannot make a tree or cloud;
    I cannot make the sea.
I'm happy that You made them, Lord,
    And that You care for me.

When I Grow Up

Sometimes it's very clear to me
    Exactly what I'm going to be:
Doctor, lawyer, merchantman,
    Astronaut or fireman.
But now and then I get confused;
    I'm not quite sure just what to choose.
I know I won't go far alone,
    So, help me, Lord, before I'm grown.

How far is far?
How cold is cold?
How young is young?
How old is old?

How rich is rich? **Questions**
How poor is poor?
How bad is bad?
How pure is pure?

There are lots of questions, God,
I don't have answers to;
So, help me always to believe
And put my trust in You.

I know You know the answers, Lord;
And, Lord, I know You care.
So, that is why I never doubt
You hear my every prayer.

Another Question

It wasn't very nice of me
    To say the things I did.
But, God, You've got to understand—
    He's such a nasty kid!

You know the one who's doing this.
    But, why? I wish I knew.
If he were me and I were You,
    O Lord, what would we do?

My Friends Won't Let Me Play

I watched my friends all playing ball;
    I wanted to play, too.
They said, "Although you wish you could,
    There is no place for you."

I felt like crying. I was sad.
    I hurt real bad inside.
So that they wouldn't see me cry
    I found a place to hide.

I thank You, Jesus, You're my friend,
    For You felt lonely, too.
Your friends ran off and left You and
    Your heart was broke in two.

But, You forgave them—every one—
    And loved them even more.
Please, help me to forgive my friends,
    For that's what friends are for.

Treasures

I found the neatest things today
    Just lying on the ground:
The feather of a pretty bird,
    An acorn, big and brown.

That bird has flown up in the sky;
    I'd like to fly along.
That acorn's just a bit like me:
    We'll both grow big and strong.

Tell me, God,
What about You?
Do You collect
Treasures too?

God Bless My Friend

I know, God, that You listen and
    You hear me when I pray.
So, can I tell You, God, what happened
    To my friend today?

He raced his bike along the road
    So fast he made a breeze
When, suddenly, he hit a rock
    And fell and hurt his knees.

He cried because it hurt a lot.
　　I cried because I care.
And now You know, dear Jesus, why
　　I come to You in prayer.

Please dry his tears, dear Jesus, Lord,
　　And let him know You care.
Please heal his knees so we can ride
　　Together everywhere.

Make Tomorrow Better

"Nobody loves me!" I said today
When Dad said words he shouldn't say.
Do You sometimes, Lord, feel this way?

Mom *yells*, "You'll *never* do things right."
I think I'll run away tonight . . .
But I'm afraid I'll die of fright.

Please, Lord, make tomorrow better.

Dear God

Dear God, You made the mountains high;
    You made the bubbly seas.
You made the pretty butterflies
    And busy bumble bees.

You made the tiny grains of sand;
    You made the big tall trees.
And then, Lord, with Your loving hands
    You made a child named me.

I Like

There are lots of things I like,
    And here are just a few:
Snakes and spiders, bats and lizards—
    God, do You like them, too?

Fun

It's fun to run and jump and roll
    Down hills so bright and green.
It's fun to swim and float and dive
    In waters cool and clean.

It's fun to walk and skip and sing
    Without a single care.
It's fun, when at the end of day
    I come to You in prayer.

DEAR PARENTS:

Prayer is one of God's special gifts to His children—both young and old. "Have faith in God," Jesus told Peter, . . . "whatever you ask for in prayer, believe that you have received it, and it will be yours" (Mark 11:22-24 NIV).

Prayer is our opportunity to talk with our heavenly Father, to ask for His forgiveness, to thank and praise Him, and to ask for His help in our lives and in the lives of others. He will hear us and will answer our prayers in His own way and in His own wisdom.

Read this little book aloud with your child. Pray often with and for your child—and for yourself. "Do not be anxious about anything," Paul told the Philippians, "but in everything by prayer and petition, with thanksgiving, present your requests to God" (4:6 NIV).

THE EDITOR